# D A T E S   W I T H   H I S T O R Y

10 November 1989 10 November 1989 10 November 1989 10 November 1989 10 November 1989 10 November 1989 10 November 1989 10 November 1989 10 November 1989 10 November 1989 10 November 1989 10 November 1989 10 November 1989 10 November 1989 10 November 1989 10 November 1989 10 November 1989 10 November 1989 10 November 1989 10 November 1989 10 November 1989 10 November 1989 10 November 1989 10 November 1989 10 November 1989 10 November 1989 10 November 1989 10 November 1989 10 November 1989 10 November 1989 10 November 1989 10 November 1989 10 November 1989 10 November 1989 10 November 1989 10 November 1989 10 November 1989 10 November 1989 10 November 1989 10 November 1989 10 November 1989 10 November 1989 10 November 1989 10 November 1989 10 November 1989 10 November 1989 10 November 1989 10 November 1989 10 November 1989 10 November 1989

# The Fall
## of the
# Berlin Wall
## 10 November 1989

# The Fall
## of the
# Berlin Wall
## 10 November 1989

CHERRYTREE BOOKS

A Cherrytree Book

This edition published in 2007
by Cherrytree Books, part of
The Evans Publishing Group
2A Portman Mansions
Chiltern Street
London W1U 6NR

VISIT OUR WEBSITE
Evans
www.evansbooks.co.uk

British Library Cataloguing in Publication Data

Williams, Brian
   Fall of the Berlin Wall. - (Dates with history)
   1. Berlin Wall, Berlin, Germany, 1961-1989 - Juvenile
   literature 2. Germany - Politics and government
   - 1945-1990 - Juvenile literature
   I. Title
   940.1'55'0878

ISBN 1842341995
13 digit ISBN 9781842344071

Printed in China by WKT Co. Ltd.

**Picture credits:**
Rex Features Limited: 11, 12, 14, 15, 17, 18, 19, 25, 26,
    27, 30, 31, 34, 35, 36, 37, 38, 39
Istockphoto: front cover
Topham Picturepoint: 20, 21, 22, 23, 24, 28, 29, 32, 33

# Contents

# The wall comes down

In 1989, crowds packed the streets in Germany to cheer and sing when a shabby strip of concrete wall in the city of Berlin was hacked down. Within two years, all that remained of this wall were a few small sections, preserved as a monument. How could the fall of a wall cause such celebrations?

The people gathered at the Berlin Wall were cheering the end of a long period of misery for one of the world's great cities. With no wall dividing it in two, Berlin was once again one city. The fall of the Berlin Wall also marked a turning point in 20th-century history – the end of the **Cold War** in Europe. Very soon Germany was one country again, after 45 years divided.

*People celebrate in Berlin as the hated wall comes down in 1989.*

# A symbol of division

For many people Berlin is a symbol of Germany as a whole. It is the biggest German city and in 1996 about 3.5 million people lived there. The city has been an important centre for German arts, education and entertainment since the 1700s. In 1871 Berlin was chosen to be the capital of the new German Empire.

During the 20th century, Berlin suffered hatred and violence. Much of the city was destroyed during

*Potsdamer Platz, a bustling square in the heart of Berlin, photographed in 1913.*

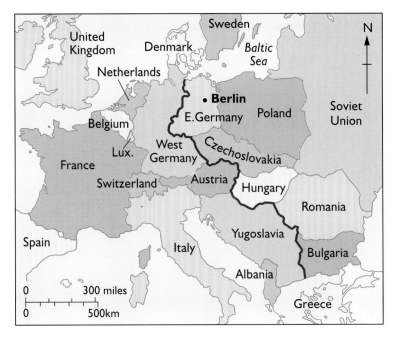

*This map shows how Germany was divided into East and West after World War II. The red line marks the Iron Curtain (see page 17).*

**World War II** (1939-1945). When peace came, the city was divided up by the countries which won the war. The Soviet Union set up a **Communist** government in East Germany, which also ran East Berlin. West Berlin was divided into three sectors, run by the British, the French and the Americans.

East Berlin was poorer than West Berlin, and over the years many East Berliners decided to move to the west. To stop people leaving, the East Germans built a wall of concrete and iron through the city in 1961. When this wall came down, on 10 November 1989, its fall marked a new era in German and, indeed, world history.

# Cheers after 28 years

Many of the people who flocked to the wall in 1989 were too young to remember Berlin before the wall was built in 1961. For 28 years, the grim wall had made travel between the two parts of the city almost impossible. People could look across the wall, but not visit friends or relatives on the other side.

In November 1989, all this changed with amazing speed. Holes appeared in the wall. Guards laid down their guns.

*People celebrate the fall of the wall at the Brandenburg Gate, a famous landmark built in 1791, which formed part of the border.*

For the first time, people were free to cross from east to west. Hundreds of thousands of people walked across a strip of ground that had once kept them apart. There were parties in the streets. Friends and relatives who had not been able to hug or shake hands for 28 years now embraced and laughed.

Many older people in Berlin during those thrilling days of 1989 had long memories. They remembered the suffering of many Berliners since 1961, when the wall was built. Some people remembered the war of 1939-45, which had ended with so much of the city destroyed.

During the 1930s the **Nazis** held many **propaganda** events in Berlin. They even tried to turn the 1936 Olympic Games into a celebration of Nazi ideas. The Nazi leader Adolf Hitler led Germany into World War II, which began in September 1939.

*World War II left Berlin in ruins. Almost everything the British and American bombs had not destroyed was smashed by Soviet tanks and guns in 1945.*

The war brought disaster for Berlin. Now 60 years after that war began, Berlin was able to look to the future. How had this revolution come about?

# Germany divided

During World War II, Berlin was bombed many times by the **Allies**. About 52,000 people were killed in **air raids**. In April 1945 **Soviet** troops captured the city. During the battle for Berlin, 100,000 people died and many buildings were smashed to rubble. On 30 April Hitler killed himself in his Berlin headquarters. Germany finally surrendered on 8 May, ending the war.

Defeated Germany was split by the victorious allies into East and West Germany. The city of Berlin was in the

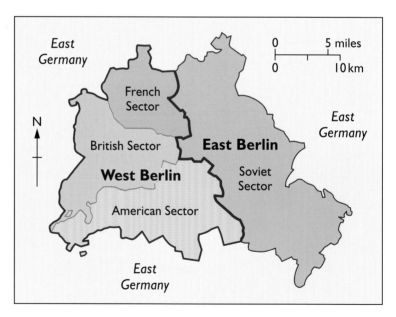

*This map shows how Berlin was split in 1945. In 1961, the Berlin Wall was built along the line separating the east (the Soviet sector), from the west (the American, British and French sectors).*

eastern part of Germany, which was under Soviet control. The Allies agreed to split the city into four areas, or sectors, and took control of an area each. The Soviets set up a Communist government in their part of Germany and allowed East German Communists to run East Berlin.

Europe was now separated by what Britain's wartime leader Winston Churchill called an **Iron Curtain**. To the east were the Communist countries under strict Soviet control, while in the west were the free **democracies**.

Soon the Soviets came into conflict with the other Allies. In 1948, the Soviets tried to cut off West Berlin from the outside world by blocking road and rail links into the city. The Allies sent in planes to carry two million tonnes of food and fuel to West Berlin, until the **blockade** was ended in May 1949.

*During the winter of 1948-49, cargo planes kept the people of West Berlin fed and warm. The Berlin Airlift flew in food, medicines and coal.*

In 1989, older Berliners could still remember that hard winter 40 years before, and other hard times since 1949. Every day, the grey concrete wall reminded them that they were prisoners in their own country.

# The wall goes up

The fact that different sectors of Berlin were run by the Soviets and the Americans meant that Berlin was a likely place for disagreements during the Cold War. This was the name given to a time of suspicion and unfriendliness between the United States and the Soviet Union between the 1940s and the 1980s. The two countries were the most powerful in the world. They did not actually fight a war, but several times they came close.

*John F Kennedy (right) talks to Nikita Khrushchev in June 1961.*

Each side had other countries as allies. Each had hundreds of **missiles**, aimed at the other. Spies tried to steal secrets. Many people in the world were afraid that there would be a **nuclear war**.

In 1961 the United States had a new president, John F Kennedy. One of his first trips abroad was to meet the Soviet leader Nikita Khrushchev, but this **summit meeting** was not a success. This was because the Soviets were worried about what was happening in Berlin. Sixty thousand

East Berliners went to work in West Berlin every day. Too many were staying, tired of the shortages and lack of freedom under Communist rule. On 8 August more than 1,700 East Germans crossed into West Berlin, to stay. The Soviet government ordered the East German government to stop the flood of people leaving for the west.

Orders went out from East Germany's Communist leader Walter Ulbricht. On 13 August, East German guards closed the **border** with barbed wire. The British and Americans protested in vain. On 20 August, the East Germans tore up streets and replaced the barbed wire with a wall of concrete blocks. East Berlin was sealed off.

*Trucks and cranes moved in to build the wall. The East Germans used factory-made blocks of concrete for speed.*

# What the wall was like

The wall was in place for so long that it had be repaired and rebuilt three times. Each time it was repaired it became bigger and tougher. The final touches were put to it in 1975 when the East Germans replaced the outer concrete blocks with new sections, topped by a tube. This created what Germans called the 'fourth generation' wall.

The outer wall, which faced West Berlin, was 3.60 m high. Each section of concrete was 120 cm thick and weighed 2,750 kg. This was only the final barrier of a fortress-like system. Behind it were sloping-sided trenches to stop vehicles being driven close to the wall.

*The wall was twice as high as a tall man and stretched for 155 kilometres.*

*Frau Frieda Schulze escaping to West Berlin from the window of her flat just inside the East German border.*

The East Germans feared that people trying to escape to West Berlin might leap from the top of a truck or even try to smash a truck through the wall. Beyond the trench line were tracks, patrolled by guards with guns and dogs. The area behind the wall was floodlit to make sure no one could hide – not that there were any hiding places.

From high watchtowers, the guards could scan long stretches of the wall. Behind the line of towers lay more obstacles: metal **tank traps** and wire fences. The Germans had a grim name for the strip of land behind the wall itself. They called it 'The Death Strip': 171 people were killed trying to cross the wall between 1961 and 1989.

# Memories of the past

During the next 25 years many more East Germans tried to escape to the west by climbing the wall. Some sneaked into empty houses near the wall, and slipped through backyards to reach it. Others swam across city canals. The wall guards shot anyone they saw making a run for freedom.

*An East German guard carries away*
*Peter Fechter's body.*

Many people never forgot one shocking incident. On 17 August 1962, Peter Fechter, a young man of 18, tried to climb the wall. Guards opened fire with a machine gun and he fell to the ground. Peter Fechter was left to die while the East German guards looked on.

From the West German side, police threw bandages, but could not reach the dying man. Later, East German police carried away Peter Fechter's body. People set up a wooden cross near the spot and left flowers. Over the years, there were many other memorials to the victims of the wall. Almost everyone in Berlin, on both sides, hated the sight of it.

In 1963 President Kennedy visited West Berlin. 'I am a Berliner,' he told a huge crowd, who applauded wildly. Unfortunately, the president actually said, '*Ich bin ein Berliner*,' which is German for 'I am a doughnut.' He should have said, '*Ich komme aus Berlin.*' People knew what he meant, however, and cheered all the same.

*In 1963 President Kennedy visited the wall. Kennedy told his audience: 'All free men, wherever they may live, are citizens of Berlin.'*

# East Germany in 1989

**B**y 1989, people in Berlin had become used to the wall. Presidents and prime ministers were taken to see it. Visitors took photos, but most Berliners seldom gave it a glance. The wall reminded everyone that Germany was divided. It had become a symbol of the Cold War.

East Berlin was the capital of East Germany. Yet by 1989 it looked shabby compared with West Berlin, with its brightly-lit streets and smart stores crowded with shoppers. In East Berlin, people still walked past desolate **bomb-sites**, in ruins more than 40 years after World War II. Most East Berliners lived in drab apartment blocks. They paid low rent and had jobs paid for by the state, but there was little in East Berlin's shops on which workers could spend their money.

*Karl-Marx Allee in East Berlin in the 1980s.*

East Germany called itself the German Democratic Republic (GDR). However, it was not a democracy at all.

People could vote for only one political party, the Communist Party. There was no freedom.

East Berlin was a favourite setting for spy stories by writers from the west. It seemed full of mystery. The border crossing on Friedrichstrasse, known as Checkpoint Charlie, featured in numerous stories and films about spies and people escaping, who made dangerous trips between east and west.

*Checkpoint Charlie was guarded on both sides. Today the guard houses used by Allied soldiers are on display in a museum.*

# Events in Moscow

In 1971 Erich Honecker took over from Walter Ulbricht as East German leader. Honecker was a long-time Communist and a loyal servant of the Soviet Union, who took his orders from Moscow.

*East German leader Erich Honecker watches East German troops parade. East Germany had a large army.*

By 1989, however, the news from Moscow was worrying. Since 1985, the Soviet Union had had a new leader, Mikhail Gorbachev. The new boss in the **Kremlin** had started a revolution of his own.

Mikhail Gorbachev had been a Communist all his adult life, but he saw now that it was time for change. He could see that the Communist countries in Europe were falling behind the west.

Factories in the Communist countries were out of date. Governments were spending too much on weapons, trying to match the United States and Europe.

*Mikhail Gorbachev (right) and Ronald Reagan began talks to end the Cold War. This alarmed the East Germans, who wondered what would happen next.*

Gorbachev became friendly with the west. He met the US President Ronald Reagan, and was on good terms with Britain's Prime Minister Margaret Thatcher. It seemed that a 'thaw' was ending the Cold War. Gorbachev wanted to solve the problems inside the Soviet Union. Smaller countries within the Communist world would have to work out solutions to their own problems.

This was bad news for the Communist leaders of East Germany. They anxiously watched the changes in Poland, Hungary and Czechoslovakia. All were moving away from Communism and towards democracy. The Iron Curtain, more than 40 years old, seemed to be rusting away.

# Voting with their feet

Most people who lived on the eastern side of the wall could not travel beyond it. Only East German officials and sports stars were free to visit the west. Yet East Germans could see what was happening in the west on television. On West German TV, people in East Germany could see the 'good life' and many were envious. Young people were keen to buy western products such as jeans, music tapes and videos.

Some began 'voting with their feet' – showing their dislike of a government they could not vote against by finding a way to leave the country. Young people headed for new lives in the west, slipping over the East German border into Austria or Czechoslovakia, and from there to West Germany. In 1988, 40,000 people left East Germany – more than three times as many as the year before.

*A young East German refugee couple in West Berlin in 1989. By the end of the 1980s, more and more East Germans were turning their backs on Communism.*

How many East Germans would leave in 1989? The worried East German government held elections in May that year. The elections were not democratic, since every **candidate** had to be approved by the Communists. The result showed that 98.77 per cent of voters backed the official candidates. In the previous election it had been over 99 per cent. So some people had expressed their disapproval of the government by not voting at all. The Christian churches in East Germany, which had helped organise opposition to the government, declared that the vote was a defeat for Communism.

*East German cars were laughed at by many West Germans. They thought them slow and smelly, alongside their smart Volkswagens, BMWs and Mercedes.*

# The tide turns

In Berlin, the wall guards were still shooting at anyone trying to cross to the west. On 6 February 1989 Chris Gueffroy was killed trying to cross the wall. However, his was the last death at the wall.

Not even the hated East German **secret police**, the Stasi, could check the protest movement now. People in East Germany had heard what was happening in the world outside. In Poland, the new free **trade union** Solidarity won the June election, defeating the Communists.

*Lech Walesa (right), leader of the Solidarity movement in Poland, at a demonstration demanding change.*

In Czechoslovakia, the writer Vaclav Havel, jailed for speaking out against Communism, was released from prison in May. Some people were even saying that the Soviet Union was about to break up.

East German **refugees** began crowding into West German **embassies**, asking for help. By 8 August, the embassy in West Berlin was full. So were those in Czechoslovakia and Hungary. Then on 10 September 1989, Hungary opened its border crossings to let refugees from East Germany travel to Austria.

*Crowds took to the streets in East Berlin to show that they were no longer afraid. They had had enough of Communism, and the government could not resist them.*

In October 1989, Mikhail Gorbachev told Erich Honecker that he must either **reform** or resign. Honecker was ill, recovering from an operation. On 7 October, Communist Party leaders met gloomily to 'celebrate' the 40th anniversary of the founding of East Germany. People were out on the streets in East Berlin, and in the cities of Dresden and Leipzig. They fought the police and chanted for freedom and democracy.

# Protest movements

**D**emonstrators refused to obey police orders to go home. The East German government was not used to such disobedience and did not know what to do. In 1961 it had sent tanks into East Berlin to guard the construction workers building the wall. Now it dared not send in soldiers. It had no friends left outside Germany.

Events in Asia influenced people too. In June 1989, people around the world watched TV pictures from China's capital, Beijing. There Communist leaders

*Chinese students called for democracy in China by crowding into Tiananmen Square in Beijing. Their protest failed.*

had sent soldiers to shoot and arrest 'freedom-protesters' in Tiananmen Square. Mikhail Gorbachev had been visiting China when the student protests began. Although he left before the 'massacre' when Chinese soldiers moved in, he heard the message. The world had blamed the Chinese government.

Gorbachev needed western friends to help his reforms. He wanted no 'massacres' in Berlin. The Soviet leader told Erich Honecker bluntly: expect no help from us, and do not order your soldiers to shoot unarmed students.

Honecker could not handle the new situation. He resigned on 18 October. East Germany's new leader was Egon Krenz,

*Erich Honecker gave up as leader of the East German government. Few people were sorry.*

but his term of office was to last only seven weeks. The East German government decided to pass a new travel law, to allow East Germans freedom to leave the country if they wished. The border with Czechoslovakia was reopened. Perhaps that would quieten things.

# People on the move

On the evening of 9 November 1989, journalists gathered at a **press conference** given by the East German leadership. Communist Party official Gunter Schabowski said that the border between east and west would be reopened 'for private trips abroad'. When would this new law come into force? 'Well, as far as I can see... immediately,' replied Mr Schabowski.

Did he mean immediately? Or was it a slip of the tongue? Whatever was meant, thousands of people in East Berlin

*Crowds of people poured through gaps in the wall as the border was opened.*

took his words as official approval for crossing into West Berlin. At Bornholmer Strasse, a crowd of East Berliners began moving towards West Berlin and at 10.30 pm the border there was opened. People gathered at the Brandenburg Gate and in the Kurfürstendamm, West Berlin's most famous shopping street.

Soon thousands of people were moving peacefully across a city which for 28 years had been divided by the wall. No one could quite believe what was happening. Masses of people were moving across Germany, heading for Berlin to see the spectacle for themselves.

Sightseers were also driving into Germany from neighbouring countries, such as Denmark and Austria. News spread fast. The roads became jammed with cars making for Berlin. Thousands of people knew

*Once the news spread, people from across Germany and from neighbouring countries drove to Berlin to see what was happening.*

that history was being made. Along the wall, the watchtowers stood empty. The guards had gone.

# Party in Berlin

Border guards no longer tried to stop the flow, but waved drivers through. In traffic jams, West German drivers carefully turned off their car engines, while East Germans left their Trabant cars running, puffing out dirty fumes.

*People hammering at the wall found that it crumbled surprisingly easily. The builders had put too much sand and water in the concrete.*

At 3 am on 10 November 1989, the streets of Berlin were still packed with people, playing music from radios, shaking hands and sharing flasks of coffee. The Potsdamer Platz, once a central square in Berlin but now a bare field, had been cut across by the wall. At 5 am, people on the western side heard the sound of drills and hammers. Holes began to appear in the concrete. Fireworks rocketed into the dawn sky. People blew whistles, sounded car hooters, boomed notes on long alpine horns. The wall was coming down.

As hundreds of people hacked at the wall, new border crossings opened like cracks in a collapsing dam. During the weekend, three million people crossed from the east to the west. On 22 December, people were again able to walk through the Brandenburg Gate, which was the centre of celebrations. The wall was fast disappearing as 'wall woodpeckers' hammered chunks of concrete out of the wall, and carried them off as souvenirs.

No longer were 197 Berlin streets blocked by the wall. The city was now one again. Berliners began a huge party to celebrate Berlin's first free Christmas since many people could remember.

*Souvenir hunters gathered pieces of the wall to take home with them.*

# Germany reunited

Once the hated Berlin Wall had come down, the next step was to reunite East and West Germany. On 7 January 1990, thousands of people formed a human chain along the old border in a call for Germany to be one again. East Germany's new leader, Hans Modrow, sent a message to Mikhail Gorbachev, asking what to do. 'Do as your people wish.' was the reply. By April 1990 Modrow had lost his job.

*People holding a banner in the human chain along the old border in January 1990. The banner reads '...that the sun shines on Germany like never before...!'*

Over Christmas, West Berlin was full of East Germans. The visitors sat in cafés, bought toys for their children and ate bananas (a luxury in the old East Germany). They had little money, but the West German government gave them free passes to concerts, museums and zoos. Most East Germans soon went home, but as winter turned to spring, Germany was still in holiday mood.

Germans realised that, almost by accident, their country was being reunited. East Germany, for 40 years a Communist stronghold, had crumbled like the wall.

After the East Germans voted in free elections, Lothar de Maizière became their first (and last) elected head of government. He called for unity with West Germany.

*A few stretches of the wall can still be seen in Berlin.*

In July 1990, East Germans began using the West German money unit, the Deutschmark. And on 3 October 1990, Germany became one country again, with Helmut Kohl as leader. There was great rejoicing. Although problems such as the inequalities between people living in the east and west had still to be tackled, the Berlin Wall had gone. In Germany, the Cold War had ended.

# Timeline

**1945**    *8 May:* World War II ends and the city of Berlin is divided.

**1948**    *24 June:* Start of the Berlin Airlift.

**1949**    *24 May:* Federal Republic of Germany (West Germany) comes into being.

**1949**    *7 October:* German Democratic Republic (East Germany) is founded.

**1952**    The border between East and West Germany is closed. Only the border between East and West Berlin remains open.

**1953**    East Germans need special passes to visit the west.

**1961**    *August:* All crossing points between East and West Berlin are closed.

**1961**    *21 August:* Gunter Litzwig is shot trying to cross the wall; he is the first of 171 known victims.

**1963**    *26 June:* President John F Kennedy visits Berlin.

**1971**    West Berlin citizens are able to visit East Berlin more freely.

**1985**    Soviet Union elects a new leader, Mikhail Gorbachev, who begins reforms.

**1987**    After seeing the Berlin Wall for himself, US President Ronald Reagan tells Mikhail Gorbachev that it must come down.

**1988**    Forty thousand East Germans leave the country.

| | |
|---|---|
| **1989** | *6 February:* The 171st death on the wall, and also the last. |
| **1989** | *8 August:* The West German mission (embassy) in East Berlin has to be closed because it is packed with East German refugees. |
| **1989** | *7 October:* People take to the streets in East Berlin and other East German cities, calling for reforms and freedom. |
| **1989** | *18 October:* East Germany's Communist leader resigns. |
| **1989** | *9 November:* The Berlin Wall is opened. |
| **1989** | *10 November:* People begin to demolish the wall. |
| **1989** | *22 December:* The Brandenburg Gate is opened so that Berliners can once more move freely across their city. |
| **1990** | *7 January:* People form a human chain along the old East-West border, calling for German unity. |
| **1990** | *July:* East Germans start to use the same money as West Germans. |
| **1990** | *3 October:* Germany is reunited. |
| **1990** | *December:* The Bundestag, the German Parliament, is moved to Berlin. |
| **1997** | Egon Krenz is sentenced to six and a half years in prison after being found guilty of manslaughter in 1989, when he ordered troops to fire on East German citizens. |
| **2000** | *9 December:* The last watchtower on the Berlin Wall is knocked down. |

# Glossary

**air raids** Attacks by planes dropping bombs on cities.

**Allies** Countries that came together to fight Germany and Japan during World War II.

**blockade** Stopping people or vehicles moving into or out of an area.

**bomb-sites** Ruined buildings or spaces where buildings once stood, after wartime bombing.

**border** The line or frontier that divides one country from another.

**candidate** Someone seeking to be elected to a political post.

**Cold War** A time of hostility between the USA and the Soviet Union, which lasted from 1945 until the 1980s.

**Communist** Someone who believes that the government should own all land and run all big businesses.

**democracy** A system of government under which people are free to vote for whoever they want, say what they like and worship as they please.

**demonstrators** Groups of people protesting in public by marching, waving flags and banners, chanting slogans or blocking roads.

**embassies** Official buildings used by ambassadors. The USA, for example, has embassy buildings in many countries.

**Iron Curtain** The name given by Winston Churchill in 1946 to the division of Europe after the Second World War, when the Soviet Union sealed off the Eastern European countries under its rule.

**Kremlin** A building in Moscow, Russia. The Kremlin was the centre of government for the old Soviet Union.

**missiles** Rockets used as guided weapons to carry explosives or nuclear bombs.

**Nazis** Members of the German National Socialist Party, which came to power in Germany in 1933 under Adolf Hitler.

**nuclear war** Waging war by using atom and hydrogen bombs to attack an enemy.

**press conference** A meeting at which a spokesperson for a government or other organisation gives out information to assembled journalists from newspapers, magazines and TV news stations.

**propaganda** Information, not always truthful, put out by a government to persuade people that its actions are right.

**reform** To make changes so as to improve things and get rid of unfairness.

**refugees** People who move from their homes seeking refuge (safety) in another country.

**secret police** A police force outside the law, used by an undemocratic government to spy on and arrest its opponents.

**Soviet** A Russian word meaning a council or assembly; the former Soviet Union (or Union of Soviet Socialist Republics) was a collection of Communist republics.

**summit meeting** A meeting between the leaders of the world's strongest nations.

**tank traps** Large blocks of concrete, or cross-barred sections of metal, placed across roads to stop tanks moving past them.

**trade union** An organisation formed by workers to protect their rights and bargain for improvements in pay and working conditions.

**World War II** The 1939-45 war fought mainly in Europe and the Pacific between the Allies on one side and Germany, Italy and Japan on the other.

# Index